41

42

44

45

47

48

49

50

52

53

54

55

57

58

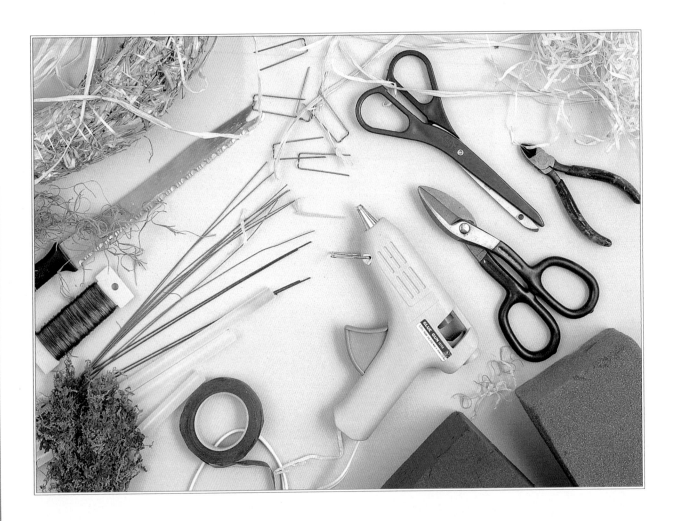

Flower arranging is universal. All the various cultures and each continuing generation contributes to the art of flower arranging. It is a constantly changing form of expression with an endless history reflecting styles, trends and the consciousness of the artist.

"Secrets of the Florist" aims to dispel doubts and uncertainties people have, to whatever degree, when it comes to expressing themselves through making flower arrangements.

Even though flower arranging has become an art form, with all its styles and standards, there is no right or wrong way to arrange flowers. If it is satisfying to assemble, feels good in the room and looks beautiful to you, the arrangement serves its purpose.

All that is needed to build confidence are a few simple guidelines on the care and mechanics of flower arranging, a few insights based on the experiences of those who have gone before you and lots of practice.

FRESH FLOWERS

Have you ever wondered why flower arrangements from the florist seem to last longer than the ones you cut and arrange yourself? Through proper selection and care, you can also create long lasting arrangements.

Whether you purchase cut flowers, grow your own or gather them from a flower-filled field, select blooms that are full of life. You can tell just by looking at them if they are going to stand tall and strut their stuff when you get them home, or droop and drop by the time you put them in a vase. Learning to recognize fresh flowers isn't difficult, but it requires practice, common sense and a good eye.

Hints

- Purchase (or cut) firm, plump flowers.

- They should be free of disease and insects.

- Look for unbroken, clean stems.

- Healthy leaves indicate a healthy plant.

- Select buds showing color.

LIFE PROLONGING TECHNIQUES

Flowers are composed of 90% water. Water keeps the flowers firm, fresh and alive. Water dissolves and transports nutrients throughout the plant. Facilitating the maximum flow of water and nutrients is the secret to longer lasting flowers.

Flowers require a healthy environment to live long and prosper. They need to be in clean containers, free from bacteria that clogs the stems and prevents circulation of water and nutrients. Vases and storage containers need to be scrubbed and rinsed with a mild solution of clorox before or after each use.

Flowers also require clean air. An arrangement placed by an open window where traffic is heavy or in a room where people are smoking will not last as long as one placed in a well ventilated environment. Just as pollutants inhibit the health and life of birds, fish and animals, they diminish the beauty and life of flowers.

Cut flowers and arrangements respond to the temperature of the water. Warm water encourages buds and closed flowers to open, and cool temperatures slow down development, adding longevity to the arrangement. Excessive hot or cold water causes plant damage. Flowers droop and wilt when placed in hot water and die quickly in very cold water.

Cut flowers require the proper kind and correct amount of nourishment. Floral preservatives are special mixtures of chemicals that have been developed and perfected to prolong the life of flowers. They contain a sugar base to keep the flower's energy level high, ingredients to inhibit the growth of bacteria, and chemicals that lower the PH and enhance water uptake.

There are many brands of preservatives available in both liquid and powder form. They can be purchased at florist shops, craft stores and at many markets. Follow the instructions carefully. Some flowers are naturally short-lived (3-4 days), while others can last two weeks or more. Using flower preservatives is a life prolonging tool for both the serious and casual flower arranger.

Arrangement contains:
China mums, Miniature gladiola
Horsetails, Pepperberries
Curly willow, Scotch broom
Sumac, Beargrass

Pre-Arranging Treatment

In order to destroy bacteria from previous plants, scrub plastic buckets (used for flowers) and vases with detergent, and rinse thoroughly. Rinse again with a mild solution of bleach; one cap full per quart of water. Bacteria from unclean containers are a primary cause of short lived arrangements. They clog the stems preventing the life-giving water from reaching the head of the flower and nourishing the complete plant. Plastic storage containers are preferable to metal ones, because the metal can interact negatively with preservatives and shorten plant life.

Fill a clean plastic storage bucket half full of bottled or purified water and the proper amount of preservatives. It is important to use purified or bottled water, because the chemicals and hard minerals in tap water block the flow of water in the stems. Allow the water to sit for a half hour, so trapped air can be released, which can also clog stems, and so it can reach room temperature.

Trim off all broken, dying, diseased, wilted or damaged flowers and leaves. This is preparation for arranging as well as cleaning off bacteria producing plant material. Remove the lower leaves from the stems.

Fill a sink, bucket or container with luke warm tap water. Warm water contains less air than cold water. Make the stem ends even, then hold them several inches underwater. Cut 1/2 to 1" from the bottom of the stems. A water droplet will form on the end of the stems and prevent air bubbles from entering and blocking the flow of water when you transfer the flowers to the storage bucket.

Flowers need to hydrate in a preservative solution to replace moisture lost during cutting and handling. Let the flowers stand and balance themselves in the storage bucket. Keep them in a cool, well ventilated place (never in direct sun) while they drink up the preservative through their freshly cut stems for six hours or so (or overnight) before placing them in their "designer home". This nourishing, treatment step maximizes solution uptake and enhances the life of the flowers.

A florist stores flowers in a special cooler that has a constant temperature, a humidifier and fans to circulate the air and moisture. Home refrigerators are not suitable for storing. They will damage flowers.

As individual flowers die, remove them to keep the arrangement looking fresh and to direct the energy of the flower to the development of emerging buds. Sometimes, if a flower has wilted, or looks a little 'tired' you can shorten the stem, remove some of the foliage, and put it in a smaller vase. Avoid getting water on the leaves and flowers. Sometimes they spot.

Special Treatment

Semi-woody stemmed flowers like hydrangeas, clematis, helleborus, poppies etc., may exude a sticky sap. The sap pollutes the water and kills the other flowers. Fresh cuts need to be cauterized in order to seal in the sap. Immerse the stem ends in boiling water for ten or fifteen seconds, or hold them over a candle flame until the ends are sealed. The water is absorbed through the cell walls of the stems. Solid woody stems that do not exude sap need to be scored or mashed to maximize water uptake.

Daffodils, narcissus, crocus and hyacinth also exude sap that is poisonous to other flowers. They need to be hydrated in separate containers for 6-8 hours before adding them to a bouquet.

Some flowers benefit from a total immersion if they have been left out of water for a few hours. They drink in moisture through their cell walls and regain their composure. Roses, peonies, lilies, wilted violets, wild flowers and especially tropical flowers rebound stronger than ever with a tepid bath before being placed in a storage container for hydration in a preservative solution.

Tulips that have curled up can be straightened by carefully placing them upright in a straight vase and adding a couple of pennies to the water.

When using 'growing' plants in an arrangement, submerge the whole plant in tap water to clean the leaves and roots. Then, hydrate them in a preservative solution before adding them to your arrangement.

Taking the time to trim off dying plant material and the leaves beneath the water line, cutting the stems under water, and allowing the flowers to hydrate in a preservative solution before arranging them in a vase, will add to the life and beauty of your arrangement.

Floral material in photo:
Protea, snowberry, eucalyptus, dogwood branches,
sterling rangl, juniper berries, cedar, plumosum

Helpful Hints
for Fresh Flowers

✻ Scour containers with a plastic pot cleaner, brush or sponge and rinse with solution of chlorine bleach.

✻ Remove all leaves and foliage below the water line. They decay quickly, have an acrid odor and distract from the design.

✻ Use distilled, reverse osmosis or de-ionized water.

✻ Cut stems under water.

✻ Cut ends of stems on a slant. Crush the ends of thick stems.

✻ Use preservatives. They enhance the colors and improve longevity.

✻ To change the water in a cut flower arrangement, place the vase in a sink or bucket, and add purified water until the vase overflows and the water runs clear. The life of the arrangement will be significantly extended by not exposing the stems to air.

MECHANICS AND TOOLS

The mainstay of any floral arrangement is the device that holds it together. The mechanics that support an arrangement need to be secure and inconspicuous. These guidelines can be used for both fresh and silk flowers. Dried flowers are light and do not require the anchoring that live and silk flowers need to hold them in place. A vase full of oasis foam is usually sufficient to support a dried arrangement.

Floral Foam

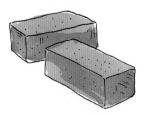

Before floral foam was available, arranged flowers were held in place with chicken wire, sphagnum moss, cut greens, pine needles or newspaper. Transporting arrangements was difficult with water sloshing and flowers moving. Flowers lasted a day or two at most. Floral foam expanded and advanced the art of floral design.

There are many types of floral foam. It comes in sticks, blocks and round shapes and in various textures and sizes. The blocks can easily be cut to the size of your container with a serrated knife.

Plastic foam is a coarse, nonporous foam. It is very sturdy and a good choice for working with large silk flowers or hanging swags. It can be cut and wedged into a container or cut smaller than the container and secured to the bottom with hot glue or pan melt glue.

Desert foam is also coarse and nonporous, but it is easier to penetrate than plastic foam. Secure to the bottom of the container with hot glue or pan melt glue.

Sahara foam is a finer variety than the previously mentioned foams. It is nonporous and needs to be secured to the bottom of the container with hot glue or pan melt glue.

Oasis foam is highly absorbent. It is best for fresh plants, because it holds water and is easy to penetrate. Leave a space between the foam and the sides of the container so water can be transferred through the foam block to the flowers.

This softer, finer foam is also preferable for standard silks and dried arrangements. It is perfect for inserting either thick or fragile stems. When using silks or dried flowers, the foam can be cut up in blocks and stuffed inside the container or shaped to fit and wedged securely in place.

PREPARING THE SATURATED FOAM

Floral foam bricks self-saturate quickly and continue to wick water to the flowers for the life of the arrangement. Water lost by evaporation or consumed by the flowers must be replaced. The saturated foam is not a substitute for water. It is best to add bottled water with preservative to your arrangement daily. As little as 10% moisture loss will cause flower wilting.

- Fill a soaking container with fresh water and a proper amount of floral preservative. (Follow the manufacturer's directions.)

- The foam should be large enough to be wedged into place and extend 1 1/2 to 2" above the rim of the vase. This allows for top and side placement of stems.

- Cut a wedge in the foam so you can add water daily. Place the cut out section at the back of the container. Don't cover it with greenery. Leave it open so you can add water.

- Allow foam to free float in a flat position. There should be enough water to fill the brick and allow it to float free when fully saturated. Don't force the saturation or air pockets will form in the foam.

- When foam is fully saturated, place in vase and tape down with waterproof tape.

Tools of the Trade

Waterproof tape is a fast, easy and all purpose method for holding either soaked or dried foam in place. It comes in two sizes: 1/4" and 1/2" wide, and three colors: white, green and clear. The tape is waterproof and pressure sensitive. Once adhered to a dry surface, it will remain firm and in place even when exposed to moisture. It sticks on pottery, metal, plastic, wood, glass, ceramics... almost anything.

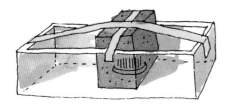

Waterproof clay is the designers' tool for positioning candles and figurines. It will also anchor dry materials like: anchor pins to each other or to vases; frogs to bases, dry foam to bases etc. It is waterproof and heat proof; can assist in positioning and holding ribbons and tissue, and will hold fruit in place for cornucopia displays. Make sure the surface is absolutely dry and free of dust or the clay won't stick.

Pan Melt Glue comes in small pellets that you can melt in an electric pan on low heat or a regular cooking pan on low heat. When the glue is melted, but not hot, dip the four corners of the floral foam into the glue, and push it onto the bottom of the container. Pan melt glue is also used to secure the ends of silk flowers in foam when making large arrangements. Dip the ends of the flower stems into the pan glue before inserting into the floral foam.

Hot Glue Gun and Glue Sticks may be used instead of pan melt glue pellets. They come in hot and lowmelt styles and in various sizes. They can be purchased at your local craft store.

Floral Stem Tape, a strong stretchable tape adheres to itself without sticking to your fingers. It's the ideal way to create corsages, bouquets, headpieces, cascades, nosegays or boutonnieres. As the tape is stretched, the adhesive material is activated. Stretch the material as you wrap it around fresh, dried or silk flower stems.

GRIDS FOR HOLDING FRESH FLOWERS IN PLACE

Flowers casually placed in a clear glass vase have been a popular style for many years. To create a more elaborate, formal arrangement, make a grid at the top of the container out of clear waterproof tape. The clear tape grid pattern is an excellent method used by professionals.

Chicken wire can also be used to hold stems in place. Bend the edges of the wire over and into the foam inside the vase. If you aren't using foam, bend the chicken wire to the inside lip of the vase, and hold it in place with a piece of 22-gauge stem wire.

Crumpled turkey wire and a pinholder provide a good grid for small stem fresh flowers. Slip the flower stems in place through the wire.

Lead crossbar slings can be purchased at florist supply stores. They are placed on the top of the container and held in place with light weight florist wire. Flowers stay upright and in place when they are placed in-between the bars.

Oasis foam sticks can be stuffed into vases and used to support flower stems and hold arrangements in place. (Scraps from larger pieces of foam can be utilized the same way.)

LACING FERNS

Lacing ferns is a quick and easy technique. Cut eight fern stems 2" shorter than the height of the vase.

1. Insert one stem in-between the last and next to last frond at the bottom of the first fern.

2. Insert the third fern in-between the last and next to last frond on the second piece of fern.

3. The fourth fern is inserted in the same location as the third piece of fern.

4. Continue lacing the ferns, inserting the fifth in the fourth and the sixth in the fifth and so on until all eight ferns have formed a grid.

Place grid securely inside the lip of the container.

SECURING YOUR ARRANGEMENT

Anchor pins (or plastic frogs) are used to secure floral foam to the bottom of the vase. Affix the pin with hot glue, waterproof clay, or double faced mounting tape. Secure the foam by pressing the dry or saturated floral foam onto the pins.

Secure a candle to your arrangement by gluing two anchor pins together, base to base. Insert one set of prongs into the foam and the other set of prongs into the candle. Anchor pins are easy and fast to use.

Foam anchor. A foam anchor has a heavy metal base with long widely spaced pins and is similar in function to anchor pins. Secure it to the bottom of the vase with waterproof clay or hot glue. If you plan to combine fresh and silk flowers, press a piece of Oasis foam onto the pins. This provides a place to insert the silk flowers.

The well pinholder is a small container with vertical pins inside. Use it in small vases for miniature or minimal arrangements.

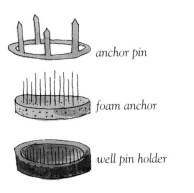

anchor pin

foam anchor

well pin holder

Candlecups are small, inexpensive containers designed to fit in a candlestick or into the neck of a bottle. Similar to a well pinholder, the candlecup is a small receptacle with needles sticking up inside. By placing a piece of foam well into the pins of the holder and securing the foam and candlecup to the candlestick or bottle with clay, florist tape or light weight wire, it can accommodate a sizeable arrangement. Candlecups are available in various sizes and are made in chrome, brass, copper, white and colored plastic.

WIRING TECHNIQUES

Having the ability to lengthen a flower stem is a great advantage in flower arranging. Also, if the flower has two or more blossoms, you can cut off the blooms and give each flower a new stem. It is a money saver and provides another possibility when arranging flowers. This technique can be used on fresh, silk or dried flowers.

Lengthening a stem

1. Place a stem wire next to the flower stem. Wrap a piece of floral tape around the top of the wire and flower stem.

2. Twirl the stem while stretching and pulling the tape in a downward angle. The tape should be tightly wrapped around the wire and flower stem without buckles or gaps along the stem.

Pierce method

To give support to a weak flower head with a thick calyx beneath the flower head, insert an 18-gauge stem wire.

1. Push one end of the wire horizontally through the calyx using half the length of the wire.

2. Bend both ends down parallel with the stem. Tape the wire starting just above the insertion.

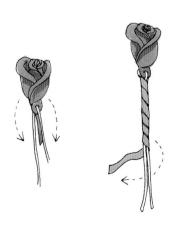

Note: A second wire may be inserted through the flower so that the two wires are crisscrossed for heavier flower heads.

Hook method

This method works well if the flower head is firmly attached to the stem.

1. Cut the flower stem an inch from the bottom of the calyx. Insert the stem wire inside the center of the stem up into the flower head until it is secure.

2. Form a hook, and pull the wire back down through the flower.

3. Tape the stem and wire tightly.

Stem supports for heavy flower heads

Flower supports add strength and flexibility to the stem allowing the flower to be gently bent.

1. Insert the end of a stem wire vertically into the base of the calyx.

2. Loosely wrap the wire around the full length of the stem in a spiral. Tape the stem to cover the wire.

Wireless taping

Wireless Taping is a perfect technique for free flowing hair pieces or corsages.

1. Cut the stem to 1" long.

2. Wrap a piece of floral tape around the top of the stem and twirl the flower in one hand while twisting the tape lightly around itself until it is as long as you want it. If you need more support, tape it again.

CONTAINERS

There is a natural relationship between a vessel and the choice of plant materials. Elegant flowers like orchids, lilies, roses, apple blossoms, amaryllis, etc., look good in 'important' containers like: curvaceous art deco vases or crystal orbs, celadon vases and glass globes. On the other hand, an arrangement of any garden or field variety placed in a sand bucket, a mason jar or an Alka Seltzer bottle can be completely charming.

Just about anything can be used as a vase for either fresh, silk or dried flowers. Start collecting containers of all shapes and sizes: shallow bowls, cylinders, compotes, goblets, trough shapes, oval containers, baskets ... look for the unusual. Choices can range from a tiny shell for a miniature arrangement to a large stone urn for an expansive room or office. Flea markets and garage sales yield a variety of bizarre and interesting vase possibilities. Clay pots are a natural for casual, all purpose containers.

Containers need to complement the setting and be consistent with the atmosphere of the room. Baskets provide an informal, country feeling. Brass, copper, silver, wrought iron and pewter add a distinctive flavor. Goblets, wine glasses, glass bricks and crystal add to the formality of an arrangement.

Be creative. Look in the plumbing department of your local hardware store. PVC pipes come in a variety of interesting shapes. They can be glued to a wooden base and used for silk and dried arrangements, or line them and use fresh flowers.

If the vessel isn't waterproof, set a glass or a paper cup inside. Floral supply houses have various sizes and shapes of pressed cardboard liners. They range from thin conical shapes to large ribbed buckets. Clear vinyl liners come in a range of sizes and can easily be trimmed to fit a variety of shapes. Valuable pots and vases should be lined with more permanent liners made out of Mylar to protect them and to avoid the need for regular cleaning.

Unglazed pottery and ceramic vases can either be treated with waterproof sealant, or they can be fitted with a plastic liner. To waterproof your container, brush on five coats of sealant, allowing each layer to dry thoroughly before applying the next one.

Lining Baskets

Waterproof baskets by lining them with heavy plastic.

1. Line the basket to the edge of the lip with heavy plastic. Cut off excess plastic around top edge of basket.

2. Cut foam to fit and place in basket.

3. Loop a #24-gauge wire through the weave at the lip of the basket, and pull the wire over the foam. Secure it to the opposite side of the basket.

Note: Foam may be soaked or dry before placing in basket.

Lining Glass Containers

When making an arrangement using foam in a clear glass vase, you can hide the foam by lining the inside of the vase with silver mylar, a light weight, polyester material. The glass becomes opaque when the lining is added.

1. Cut a piece of Mylar slightly larger than the container. If the Mylar is large enough to cover the outside, it will fit the inside.

2. Place a soaked piece of floral foam into the Mylar lined vase.

3. Fill the container with water. Pull up gently on the excess Mylar around the edge of the vase. Leave it as a ruffle or trim the Mylar even with the edge of the container.

Preparing Containers for Arrangements

Bowls. Shape some foam to fit the bowl. Using waterproof clay, secure a plastic frog on the bottom of the bowl. Impale the foam on the frog.

Dishes. Mound the top of the foam using extra pieces taped together if necessary. Using a strong glue, hot glue or pan melt glue, adhere the foam to the dish.

Tall Vases. Using Oasis foam, stuff the entire vase with pieces of foam that extend about an inch above the top of the vase.

Spherical vases. Insert a loose ball of chicken wire inside, and stretch it until it pushes against the interior surfaces.

Glass containers. Adhere plastic frogs to the bottom of the glass container with waterproof clay. Cut the foam about 3/4" smaller on all four sides of the vase. Secure the foam on the frogs. If you are making a silk or dried arrangement, fill the edges of the vase with potpourri, Spanish moss or sphagnum moss. Fill the edges of the vase with pebbles, marbles or sand to hide the foam for a fresh arrangement.

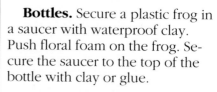

Bottles. Secure a plastic frog in a saucer with waterproof clay. Push floral foam on the frog. Secure the saucer to the top of the bottle with clay or glue.

Make Your Own Containers

Hay covered containers are easy to make and can transform any receptacle into a charming vase. You won't find hay in a craft store, but depending on where you live and what time of year it is, hay shouldn't be too difficult to locate.

1. Gather a basket, vase or can, some long strips of raffia and enough hay to give the container a thick covering.

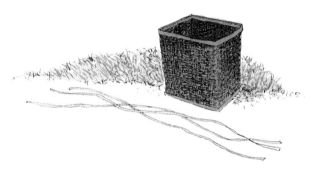

2. Place the hay on top of the two long strips of raffia, and roll the container, using the raffia to hold the hay in place.

3. Tie the raffia tightly adding additional strips if needed. Trim off the top.

Miniature arrangements are a delight to make, receive as a gift or keep for yourself. Make them out of found objects. The hardware store has bins of turned wooden legs (short and tall) and wooden knobs. They make interesting bases for containers. Stack them like blocks and glue them together. Glue a small container on top for your arrangement. Spray them with acrylic paint, add touches of lace and ribbon.

After you glue your found objects together, spray with white (or any color you choose) and paint designs on them. When they are dry, spray with a coat of varnish. It gives a nice shine and a finished look.

Cover containers with ribbon, lace, fabric and trim. These were made out of chopped olive cans. Wash thoroughly, and spray with white acrylic paint. Secure ribbons and lace with hot glue.

Small color spots can be used in may ways. Place them with live plants in a window garden, set them in clusters in the bathroom or on shelves and tables.

Wedge a piece of floral foam in a 2 1/2" flower pot, and cover it with a little moss. Cut some leaves from a greenery bush, leaving a 2" stem. Insert in the middle of the foam. Add a few flowers for color and a thin ribbon around the top of the pot to add a finishing touch.

Create a container within a container

If your container is made of glass, surround the floral foam with potpourri, moss, and little flowers, or wrap the foam in raffia or colored tissue before placing it into the vase. Bury the foam in sand or pebbles and surround it with interesting twigs and sticks. The transparent vase becomes part of the design.

Bases

A base of slate or a crosscut piece of wood can be used as a platform to work from and can also contribute to the shape and style of the design. For a more formal arrangement the wood can be covered with an elegant fabric. A sturdy fabric such as burlap or a cotton weave can be used for a less formal arrangement. Polished or unpolished wood, cork, bamboo, clear plastic sheets, blocks of plexiglass and polished marble are all excellent and versatile materials for bases.

Instructions for project at right can be found on page 49

Dried Flowers

DRIED FLOWERS

Like silk and fresh flowers, dried flowers, leaves, seed heads and pods have a charm of their own. They allow us to combine flowers from different seasons providing endearing, ever-lasting bouquets. When added to ribbons and hats, they remind us of fragrant, warm, sunny days and special times in our life.

Pressed flowers can be glued to special papers and used as cards or stationery. They can be arranged into patterns and pictures, glued in place and framed. Exotic pods, plants and leaves can be preserved for unusual and extraordinary arrangements.

GROWING YOUR OWN

Growing your own flowers will give you the added enjoyment of appreciating them while they are fresh as well as dried. You don't need a large area to grow enough plants for several large arrangements. Plan your garden so you can enjoy it year around by planting evergreens, deciduous plants (they loose their leaves in the fall), annuals and perennials.

By planting a variety of kinds and colors of flowers and plants, you will have enough materials for many interesting projects. Plant rows of flowers in your vegetable garden. Herbs are easy to grow, and can be planted in pots and window boxes. They transform simple cooking into gourmet dishes, and they delicately scent a room when dried and used in a wreath or an arrangement.

HARVESTING

Success depends not only upon the preserving process, but also on picking the fresh plants at the right time. Cut flowers when the heads feel firm and before they come into full bloom. Enjoy cut roses as they open, and just before they reach full bloom, remove them from the water and hang them upside down to dry.

Flowers like delphinium, larkspur, foxglove, lupin etc., should be gathered when the lower buds are flowering, but the very top ones have not yet opened. Choose perfect plants. Pick flowers when they are at their peak or a little before. Mature flowers will fall apart during the drying process.

Avoid cutting before the morning dew has dried off, after a rainfall and before the midday sun has begun to wilt them. Gather more than you need, to allow for breakage. Cut the stems at an angle with sharp clippers, knife or scissors.

AIR DRYING

The easiest way to dry flowers is to tie them in small bundles with twine, raffia or ribbons, and hang them upside down, out of direct sunlight, in a warm, well-ventilated place. Use wall hooks, poles or wires placed at least 6" from the ceiling. Stagger the heads to allow plenty of air to circulate. This prevents mildew and rot. Bunches should contain one type of flower.

Sturdier flowers like bells of Ireland, roses, statice, gypsophila, yarrow and larkspur dry well using the air dry method. Strip off most of the leaves as soon as possible. The leaves retain moisture and will slow down the drying process. Dry large flowers like dahlias and sunflowers individually. The air drying process usually takes two to three weeks.

The flower heads of many of the straw flowers are too heavy for the dried stems

to support them. Cut the stems and wire them before hanging out to dry.

If a flower head falls off during the drying process, hot glue a floral stem wire to the head or calyx of the dried flower, and cover the wire stem with florist tape.

Adding Wire Stems

1. Cut each flower head from the spray so that the stem is approximately 1 1/2" long.

2. Using 20-gauge wire, cut the wire to the desired length, allowing extra for bending and for the part of the stem to be inserted into the floral foam. Bend the tip of the wire with pliers to form a 'shepherd's hook'.

3. Hook the wire around the calyx, where the flower head joins the stem, and squeeze tightly with needle nose pliers.

4. Wrap green floral tape over wire from top to bottom.

5. Hang flowers to dry.

Grasses, moss, lichen, bamboo, fungi and leafy branches dry well when laid flat on an absorbent surface like cardboard, newspaper or even wooden floorboards. Whole branches, ferns, bracken and spiky leaves can also be dried this way.

Arrange material in a single layer on several pieces of newspaper. Don't overlap the material. The leaves will shrink a little, but they will retain their color and natural shape on the stalk, (which they will not do if they are hung upside down or dried upright).

Make a simple shelf of coarse gauge chicken wire for air drying heavy headed plant material such as: globe artichokes, large onion seed heads, protea and large thistles. Each plant has a home in a hole. Provide enough room beneath to allow the stems to hang freely.

Many tall grasses dry well standing up in a dry vase. Seal pampas grass, bulrushes and other seed heads by spraying them with hair spray or a similar fixative before drying. This keeps them from shedding.

WATER DRYING

Strip off most of the leaves and place the flower stem in 2" of water. Place it in a warm place out of direct sunlight. The water is absorbed and evaporated as the flower dries. Hydrangeas, heathers, hybrid delphiniums, acacia, gypsophila and yarrow dry well this way.

PRESERVING

Miniature oak, maple, magnolia leaves, copper beech, laurel, pin oak, and eucalyptus can be dried successfully by letting them stand in a solution of glycerine and water. The color of the leaves usually changes from green to a beautiful, rich shade of greenish brown. Gather the foliage in the summer while the sap is still rising.

Cut the base of each stalk at a sharp angle so the plant will take up the mixture quickly. Remove the bottom leaves, so that only the stem rests in the solution. Hardwood stems should be hammered and split to increase their intake capability.

Stand the plants in water for a couple of hours so they are refreshed. Then, make the glycerine solution using 40% glycerine and 60% very hot water. Stand the plants in a container with 3-4" of the mixture in the bottom. Leave in a cool, dark place for about 10 days.

As the glycerine is absorbed through the plant, it becomes 'embalmed'. It is preserved, yet still supple. Material treated with glycerine lasts indefinitely, and can be dusted or wiped with a damp cloth without risk of breakage

OVEN DRYING

Compact flowers like marigolds, chrysanthemums, cornflowers and zinnias dry well in a fan assisted, convection oven. Non-ventilated ovens are not appropriate, because they generate too much moisture.

The material must be dried at a very low temperature (100 degrees), over many hours. The flowers are slotted through holes in a wire mesh rack leaving room for the stems to dangle below. The time required depends upon the density of the flowers. Check often to make sure the oven doesn't get too hot.

MICROWAVE DRYING

Herb's can be successfully dried in the microwave and stored for future use. Cut perfect leaves, and remove any foreign material. Don't pre-wash. Place on a paper towel, don't overlap, and heat on high for one minute. If still moist, change the paper towel, and repeat the process until herbs are dry. Allow herbs to become room temperature before storing in a tightly covered container.

Sunflowers, chrysanthemums, roses, asters, zinnias... any compact flower dries well and retains its color and shape when dried in the microwave. Fresh, perfect, half-open flowers are preferred. Each flower and leaf has its own unique drying time, so avoid placing different varieties in the microwave at the same time.

In principle, all flowers can be dried, but flowers with thick petals such as: clematis vitelba, hyacinth or magnolias do not dry well, even in the microwave.

MICROWAVING WITH SILICA GEL

Silica gel is a highly absorbent desiccant. When combined with microwave drying, flowers retain their vivid color. The crystals also provide support and keep the flowers from re-absorbing the released moisture.

Choose flowers that are partially open. Petals fall off if the flower is in full bloom. Buds will not dry well, because the silica gel cannot find its way to the tightly closed petals in the center of the flower. Some small buds can be dried however; experiment. Leaves are dried separately, because they dry faster.

Select simple structured flowers like marigolds for your first flower. Allow the dew to dry on the petals and leaves before placing in the microwave. Most flowers hold their shape better if dried face up. Branches with multiple blossoms, however, should be dried lying flat.

1. Cut the stem 1" below the head. Insert a wooden toothpick into the base of the flower, and trim the toothpick to 1/2" long. (After the flower is dried, a stem wire can be placed beside the toothpick and taped with floral tape to form a strong, flexible stem.)

2. Layer 1 1/4" of silica gel crystals on the bottom of your container with a spoon. Stand the flowers upright in the crystals. Space them out so they are not touching the sides of the container or each other. Gently cover the flowers completely with another 1 1/4" of silica gel. Place the container on a rack or elevated in the middle of the microwave.

3. Because of the variation in microwaves and the amount of moisture in plants, it is impossible to give exact guidelines for drying time. Generally speaking, drying time for one or more flowers in about 1/2 pound of silica gel, is 2 to 2 1/2 minutes; 2 1/4 pounds of silica gel, 5 to 6 minutes; and 3 1/2 pounds of silica gel, 6 to 7 minutes.

If you are not sure of the temperature setting on your microwave, insert a nonmetal thermometer between the flowers in the silica gel, positioned so you can read it through the door. Stop 'cooking' when the silica gel reaches 300 degrees.

4. Remove a few crystals to see if the petals are still moist. If they are, re-cover the flower and microwave in 15 second timings until the flower is dry.

5. To prevent released moisture from being re-absorbed by the flowers after they are dry, put a lid over them and allow them to remain standing in the microwave for 10-15 minutes with the door open. They will continue drying even after the oven is finished.

6. Gently remove the flowers from the silica gel. Brush off the crystals with an artist's brush. If some parts of the stem or flower are still damp cover those parts with more silica gel, and return the flower to the microwave. Repeat the covered standing time.

7. When the flowers are completely dry they are ready for wiring.

PRESERVING WITH DESICCANTS

Although drying with desiccants, such as silica gel or a mixture of borax and corn meal, can be the least predictable way to preserve flowers and foliage, the results can be dazzling and lifelike.

The desiccant must be completely dry before you begin. Warm it in the oven for a half hour before placing a layer in the bottom of a plastic storage box.

Cut off the flower heads leaving 1" stems (for future wiring). Pour a blanket of silica gel or an equal mixture of borax and cornmeal over each flower. Separate the petals carefully with a toothpick as you pour. When each flower is completely covered, put a tight fitting lid on the container and store in a dry place. Check in 4-5 days to see if the flowers are papery and dry. If not, re-cover with silica gel and the lid of the box, and check again in a couple of days.

If they are left too long, they become brittle and dark. So, check frequently. When dry, remove the desiccant with a soft brush and wire the fragile stems.

Restoring Silica Gel

Preheat the oven to 300 degrees. Sift through to remove as much plant debris as possible, and spread a single layer of used silica gel on the bottom of a shallow pan. Place in the oven. Stir from time to time until it regains its original blue color. Store after cooling in an air tight container.

PRESSING

Delicate flowers and leaves like maidenhair fern, pansies, prim rose flowerets, lace cap hydrangeas, anemones, snowdrops, clematis, hellebore and violets can be placed between sheets of waxed paper and inserted between the pages of an old telephone book. Spread them out so they are not touching. The waxed paper keeps the flora from sticking to the pages of the book. Pile some extra heavy books on top of the phone book to add some pressure. In two to three weeks the plants will dry, and the weight of the books will press the flowers and leaves into beautiful shapes.

Whole branches, ferns, bracken and spiky leaves can also be dried this way. Arrange the material in a single layer on wax paper over newspaper, no overlapping. Cover with another layer of wax paper and some more newspaper. Then, put the parcel under some pressure. The length of time material takes to dry depends on how porous it is. Check after ten days.

Storing Dried Flowers and Plants

The safest way to store dried flora is in a long, shallow cardboard box. Poke holes in it so the air can circulate, and add small packets of desiccants to absorb any moisture. Wrap bunches of like-flowers in tissue or newspaper, and lay them in a head and foot arrangement.

Don't overcrowd. Label the box, and store where the temperature is relatively constant. Very delicate material can be stored hanging upside down with an umbrella of tissue paper to protect the flowers from light (which fades) and dust.

Ready for use

- Glycerine dried flowers can be misted with water and allowed to stand for 30 minutes to regain their suppleness.
- Statice may be stored in the refrigerator for a few hours to regain a fresh look.
- Dried roses can be lightly steamed to expand the flower heads so you can fan out the leaves and petals.

COMBINING DRIED AND SILK FLORALS

Just as fresh and silk flowers can be combined when making arrangements, silk and dried materials can also be used together. Adding baby's breath to an arrangement of silk flowers can have a softening effect, and dried star flowers or statice can add texture and color. Preserved eucalyptus, dried larkspur or dried bird of paradise leaves can be used as 'line flowers'. 'Filler material', flowers with fine stems, can be bundled into single units with twine or light weight floral wire before being used in a design.

BASIC DRIED GLOBES AND WREATH

Ornamental Globes

1. Snip heads from dried materials leaving ½" stems. Cover ⅓ of a 3" floral foam ball with tacky glue.
2. Push the flowers or seed heads close together into the glue-coated foam. Repeat the process of gluing and pushing until the ball is covered.
3. Sprinkle finished globe with potpourri oil and place in a basket or your favorite bowl.

Fantasy Wreath

1. Pour tacky glue onto a plastic plate. Apply liberally to a grapevine wreath with a paint brush.
2. Press sphagnum moss into the glue until the entire wreath is covered. Allow to dry.
3. Glue dried flower heads and a raffia bow onto moss.

BASIC DRIED ARRANGEMENT

Fill the container with the softest, densest floral foam. The stems require a soft foam in order to penetrate. Allow the foam to extend an inch or so over the edge of the container so you can add stems horizontally.

1. Establish the overall shape of the arrangement with filler flowers like: heather, huckleberry, mini daisies, gypsy grass, broom bloom, and/or preserved gyp.

2. Accentuate the overall shape of the arrangement with line flowers like: liatris, larkspur, delphinium or purple sage.

3. Highlight the arrangement with the focal flowers last so they don't get lost in all the dried material. Use mums, carnations, roses, or any larger flower. In dried arrangements there is usually an abundance of material and focal flowers are spread throughout the design.

Note: The dried arrangement can be something you keep transforming by adding new beautiful touches, changing the container or trimming the length of the stems.

Instructions for the project below can be found on page 50.

DRIED FLORAL TREES

Small trees made with real branches (for the trunk) and cone-shaped dry foam (for the tree) are very easy to construct. Purchase some plaster of Paris (not pre-mixed), a container, a cone shaped piece of foam, some moss (any style) and floral pins to secure the moss. Look in your garden for a small, straight branch for the trunk of the tree. Use whatever dried flora you prefer to decorate it, and secure your decorations with hot glue.

1. Line a pot with slivers of floral foam. The plaster of Paris expands as it sets. The foam acts as a cushion and keeps the pot from cracking.

2. Mix enough plaster of Paris and water to fill the pot 2/3 full. Make sure the slivers of foam stay in place as you spoon the mixture into the pot.

3. Insert the trunk, making sure it rests on the bottom of the pot. Turn the pot and adjust the trunk until it looks straight from all angles. When you are happy with it, add some more plaster up to 1" from the rim of the pot.

4. When the plaster is dry, push the foam cone onto the 'trunk', and cover it with moss. Use floral pins to hold the moss in place.

5. Decorate the tree by hot gluing dried flowers and leaves to the moss. Cover the top of the plaster with glue and add the moss.

Note: Smaller trees do not require anchoring with plaster of Paris. Wedge a piece of foam snugly into the pot. Insert the branch in the cone and the other end of the branch in the foam in the pot. Cover the cone with moss and decorations, and cover the foam in the pot with moss.

SWAGS AND GARLANDS

Creating a long graceful swag to adorn a banister, doorway, fireplace, wall, etc., or making an unusual, beautiful garland to place lovingly around a special painting or photograph is a very satisfying project to make. It can be a reminder of special times and events. A wire based swag is flexible, strong and easy to assemble.

1. Unroll enough reel wire for the length of the project. Don't cut the wire. Make a loop at the end (for hanging).

2. Wire a small bouquet, and trim the ends even.

3. Place the bouquet on top of the wire (cover the loop), and bind it in place with the attached reel of wire. Pass the reel under the last wire loop and pull tight.

4. Make a second bouquet like the first one, and place it on the wire with the tips covering the wire around the first bouquet. Bind the second bouquet in place as you did the first one. Repeat the procedure until the project is complete.

HANGING A WREATH

1. Twist a circle in the middle of a piece of medium gauge stem wire.

2. Push the ends of the wire into the covered wreath base.

3. Secure the ends by wrapping them around each side of the back of the wreath.

SILK FLOWERS

'Silk' flowers is the generic name for several styles of silk, polyester and paper flowers. There are 'silk' flowers that have the appearance of freeze dried blooms. Made of soft, silky fabrics in beautiful muted colors, they provide a charming, decorative touch to any room. There are soft, subtle shades of paper and vinyl flowers that have a sturdy appearance and velvety petals. They look and feel similar to fresh blooms.

'Silk' flowers and greenery come in a wide range of styles and prices. They can vary from 49 cents or less to 50 dollars or more for a single flower. The fineness of the fabric, the complexity of the style; whether they are hand wrapped and assembled or machine made, all determine the quality and availability of the flowers and greenery.

FLORAL FOAM FOR SILK ARRANGEMENTS

The softer, more absorbent floral foams are perfect for most arrangements. Both thick and delicate stems penetrate easily. Also, the more absorbent foam is necessary if you are combining fresh with silks.

✿ When the instructions for a project call for floral foam, examine the size and shape of your container to decide how many pieces of foam you will need. If your container is glass and you want to camouflage the foam by surrounding it with moss or raffia, factor that into your decision.

✿ When combining fresh and silks, anchor the foam to the bottom of the vase. Secure a floral prong to the bottom of the vase, and push the foam onto the prongs, or hot glue the foam to the container. Then, when you add water, the foam won't float to the top, and topple your arrangement.

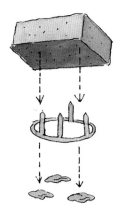

✿ If you are making a tall arrangement in a shallow container, hot glue the foam to the base or glue the prong and add the foam. In smaller containers, the foam block can be wedged inside or the container can be stuffed with pieces of absorbent foam. If the foam isn't secure, the arrangement won't be secure.

✿ As in fresh arrangements, allow the foam to extend an inch or so above the top of the container, so you can insert stems out the sides in graceful angles.

✿ Cover the secured foam with moss...either sphagnum or Spanish and secure the moss with floral pins, a "U" shaped metal pin. This is standard procedure. But sometimes, in a large arrangement, with many stems and leaves, it is easier to insert the stems directly into the foam and add the moss in-between the stems, where the foam shows, after the arrangement is complete.

✿ Line the bottom of baskets with newspaper before wedging a piece of foam inside and covering it with moss. This will prevent pieces of moss and foam from falling through the basket onto your furniture.

WORKING WITH GREENERY

Smooth the leaves and separate the branches. Usually, any crushed leaves can be straightened out by hand. If not, wrinkled leaves can be restored by steaming them with a standard steam iron. Set the temperature at the lowest setting for steam. Test the corner of a leaf before you begin to steam out the wrinkles.

The best way to separate the long stems on large bushes is to start from the ends. (Be sure to snip the wires that wrap the stems together first.) Separate the tips of the stems and gently pull them apart. If a few leaves pop off in the process, attach them as you go or save them. You can always use extra leaves for a hat or a mini arrangement. Pull the stems from the main branch in the direction they are constructed. That way, the shape of the spray is preserved, and you don't end up with stems crossing over in all directions. If the bush has some adjustable leaves slide the sets of leaves up, so they are evenly spaced.

Look at the overall shape of the bush before you begin your arrangement. Mix it with some other leaves to see which ones look good together. If the longer stems don't work for you, cut them off, and plan to insert them as single stems. If the stems are too short, wrap a stem wire around the end of the stem, and insert the wire into the foam.

If you are using sprays of leaves like eucalyptus, or bushes of leaves like coleus, insert the whole stem or cluster of stems into the foam before snipping off a branch or leaf. Sometimes it is easier to see what needs to go once it is in the arrangement.

Different shades of color (especially greens) are a lot easier to see in natural light. When mixing greens it is essential to choose colors, leaf sizes and shapes that go well with each other. If you aren't sure, take them outside where you can see the subtle differences in the colors.

Some greenery can look a little 'leggy' when there is a lot of stem between the leaves. To avoid a 'too perfect' looking stem with all the leaves evenly spaced, cut stems from other greenery with smaller leaves, and wind it around the stems in-between the larger leaves. It fills out the long stems that add grace to an arrangement. Small ivy sprays with the soft

wiry stems can be cut from the spray, leaving the stems as long as possible, and used for this purpose.

When making an arrangement that is predominantly leaves, using flowers as accents, insert the foliage first. Establish the shape of the arrangement with the leaves, and then add the flower accents.

THE VERSATILE GREENS

Hot glue a piece of foam to a wooden base. Cover the foam with moss, and secure the moss with floral pins. Add some rocks, sand and greenery, and you have an 'environment' for your dining room or coffee table.

Hot glue some leaves and a few small flowers to a piece of driftwood, and you have a unique, charming centerpiece or mantle arrangement.

GREENERY WREATHS

Lay your Styrofoam wreath flat on a table, and cover it with moss. Secure the moss with floral pins. Then, hang the wreath on the wall to add the greenery. It is easier to see where you need to add more leaves, flower accents etc., when you are face to face with your wreath.

Green garlands are perfect for making wreaths. Unwind the garland and lay it loosely, alternating back and forth, around the wreath. Cut off the excess garland, and attach the greenery to the wreath with floral pins. Cut up the excess garland to fill in any sparse areas. Add fruit, tiny flowers...anything you like, or leave it green.

If you choose to add berries or single flowers to a wreath, and the stems are too soft to penetrate the foam, wrap a wire around the end of the stem, double it over, twist it, and insert it in the wreath base. Use floral pins when adding multiple flowers and berries.

CENTERPIECES

Centerpieces should be short, and candles should be either very short or very tall, so they don't block conversation or isolate guests . The container should be in character with the table setting. Pottery looks better with wicker and plastic; silver and crystal look better with fine china. If the dishes are colorful, select most of the arranging material in the hue that appears in the smallest quantity in the china.

The shape of the arrangement should echo the shape of the table: round arrangements with round or square tables, oblong arrangements with rectangular tables.

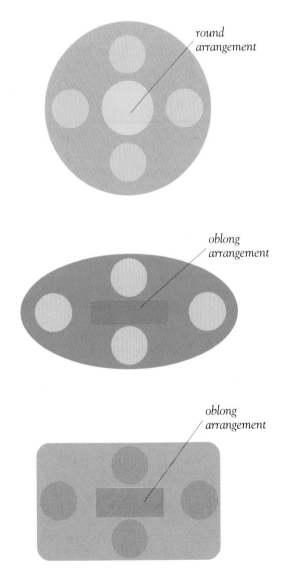

round arrangement

oblong arrangement

oblong arrangement

31

WORKING WITH SILK FLOWERS

Use wire clippers to shorten stems and floral picks to lengthen them. Floral picks are wooden sticks that come in different lengths, and have wire loops at the top. By wrapping the wire loop around the short stem you have the additional length of the wooden stick to use as the flower stem.

Light stems will stay wherever they are placed in the foam, but taller, heavier stems may tend to swivel. This can be avoided by slitting the tape which binds the multi-wired stem, and separating the wires into a 'fork'. The double stem is then pushed into the foam.

For a large, single wire stem, that tends to shift in the foam, another wire can be twisted around the base of the stem to form an extra 'leg'. Cover it with floral tape for added support. Or, if the stem is not too tall, you can add some hot glue in the hole where the stem pokes into the foam.

Silk bushes, pre-formed silk bouquets and greenery can be cut into single stems for individual arrangements, or smaller projects like: corsages, headpieces and boutonnieres.

GUIDELINES FOR MAKING SILK ARRANGEMENTS

✻ Gently bend the flowers and leaves with your thumbs and forefingers into soft, natural curves before inserting the flowers and leaves into the foam. Separate the branches and smooth the petals.

✻ For a more natural, relaxed look, that is beautiful from any side, turn the arrangement as you add flowers and leaves, and insert stems at angles so flowers face different directions.

✻ Allow breathing space between flowers to prevent a crushed or crowded look.

✻ Use flowers in different stages of development, from bud to full bloom. Place the buds at the top of the arrangement and further out from the full flowers to create a natural look and feeling.

✻ When using tall, opaque containers, Oasis foam (green) can be cut into small pieces and stuffed inside the container to hold the flowers in place.

✻ Fillers such as sand, kitty litter or even bird gravel can be used to raise the floor of the container and add ballast.

✻ When using clear containers, add marbles, layers of interesting rocks, raffia, potpourri or moss to hide the foam, hold the stems in place and/or add weight to the arrangement.

✻ Position a container with three legs to show one leg directly in front.

✻ Dip stems in pan glue, white glue or hot glue before inserting them in the foam for more secure designs.

CLEANING SILKS AND DRIED FLOWERS

Silks can be sloshed around in warm, sudsy water in the bath tub or sink, and they can be damp dusted. But, the easiest way to clean silks (and dried flowers) is with an ozone safe aerosol spray for silks and dried flowers. They are inexpensive, and they restore color as well.

Paper flowers can be dusted with a feather duster or blown with a hair dryer on a low setting. Paper flowers can be reshaped by lightly steaming them with a travel iron or a steam iron on the lowest setting for steam.

LINE, FOCAL AND FILLER FLOWERS

Some flowers are long and thin, some are round and big and some are smaller, multiple-blossomed flowers. The long ones are called 'line' flowers, the round ones, 'focal' flowers and the smaller blossoms are called 'filler' flowers. They provide the necessary ingredients for the basic bouquet. The line flowers are inserted first, to establish the direction and shape of the arrangement. Then, focal and filler flowers are added.

Line flowers stand tall and have many blossoms close to the stem. They are 'showy' flowers like: snapdragons, delphiniums and stock. In the illustration, two snapdragons are used to establish the line of the design.

Focal flowers are single stem, compact florals that command the attention of the viewer and are placed close to the center of the arrangement slightly above and below the lip of the container. They add weight and volume to a design and are usually round like carnations, roses, lilies and peonies.

Filler flowers have clusters of individual flowers on a single stem or flower head. Some fillers have multiple leaves and feathering blooms. They are transitional flowers and fill spaces between the line and focal flowers. Statice, dianthus, denzia, pom-poms and waxflowers are examples of filler florals.

EIGHT BASIC FLORAL DESIGNS

Horizontal arrangements are often used for centerpieces, tables, window sills...anywhere a long arrangement is suitable. Horizontal arrangements can suggest a natural growth pattern by using simple lines of flowers.

1. Using a relatively shallow container (or a piece of floral foam), anchor foam and position sprays of line flowers to establish the shape of the design.

2. Insert focal flowers in the middle so they gently droop over the lip of the container on both sides, reach towards the line material and extend on either side of the middle. Leave room for filler flowers.

3. Fill in and around focal area with filler flowers and foliage.

Vertical arrangements offer a continuous line of movement upward. Iris, arum lilies, calla lilies, larkspur, eucalyptus and bird of paradise are often used. Tall, slender designs are excellent where space is limited.

1. Secure foam in a vase. Cut the stems of the tallest flowers or leaves to reach three or four times the height of the vase.

2. Place the focal flowers vertically within the diameter of the vase.

3. Fill in the areas as needed with filler flowers.

Triangular arrangements are pleasing in traditional or contemporary settings. The shape may be equally balanced on each side or asymmetrical with one point of the triangle extending further than the other. A variety of sizes, shapes, textures and types of flowers can be used. Stems radiate from a central area with paler and smaller flowers and leaves at the outer edges and deep colored or brighter blooms near the center. Sometimes one half of the arrangement mirrors the other.

1. Determine the vertical height and horizontal width with the smallest line flowers and leaves. Make the height higher than the width.

2. Position the largest focal flowers in the heart of the arrangement and slightly lower to give weight and balance.

3. Fill in with the filler flowers and foliage keeping within the triangular shape.

Oval arrangements have a similar appearance from all sides. They can be constructed in a formal way with larger blooms centrally placed and smaller ones echoing around the edges. Turn the vase as you add the flowers. If the vase isn't stable, tape it in place with floral tape on a lazy susan so it doesn't topple over while you are arranging the flowers.

1. Determine the height with line flowers, then frame in the outer edges of the oval shape with light colored flowers and foliage.

2. Place the largest, strongest or brightest flowers in the focal area.

3. Fill in around the larger flowers and leaves with the filler flowers.

Minimal arrangements make use of space as a design element, and styling is done with an economy of materials. They present meditative and dramatic understatements. Arrangements can have groups of similar flowers or a variety of blooms and textures to create a mood or atmosphere.

1. Adhere foam to container. Insert vertical line flowers to determine the height, and secure the horizontal line flowers to give the basic outline of the arrangement.

2. Place the focal flowers.

3. Fill in with filler flowers as needed.

The lazy 'S' or 'Hogarth Curve' was named for a painter, William Hogarth, who loved to paint flowers in the shape of graceful curves.

1. Anchor the foam securely. Bend the stems gently into graceful curves and insert them in place so they balance.

2. Add the focal flowers following the lines of the upper and lower curves.

3. Cluster filler blossoms and foliage around the central flowers maintaining the rhythm of the 'S'.

Free Standing arrangements are similar to ovals in the universality of their shape and their circular design. But ovals have a gently rounded arc at the top, and free standing arrangements come to a definite point like a Christmas tree. They include an abundance of flowers and can be placed to show from all sides.

1. Fill a shallow container with foam that extends one inch over the top. Secure the foam with hot glue, floral clay or floral tape. Define the shape of the design with the line flowers and leaves.

2. Place the focal flowers and leaves, turning the vase as you go, so all the sides are even.

3. Add filler flowers to integrate the design.

THE BASIC BOW

These directions show how to make a bow using three yards of ribbon. By adjusting the streamer length, loop size and number of loops, the same technique can be used to make any size bow.

1 Measure 14" for the first tail. Squeeze the ribbon together and hold it with your thumb and forefinger.

2 With the right side of the ribbon facing out, make a loop on one side using 8-9" of ribbon. Pinch the ribbon together, and hold it with your thumb and forefinger.

3 Make a full twist of the ribbon, and make a loop toward the other side.

4 Continuing to hold the ribbon at the pinched area with your thumb and forefinger, make a slightly smaller loop on top of the first one. The second, third and fourth sets of loops should be slightly smaller than the first set. Be sure to fully twist each loop so that the right side of the ribbon is always facing out.

5 To complete the bow, twist the remaining ribbon around your thumb to make the center loop (or 'button'). Adjust the tail so the right side of the ribbon is facing out like the first tail. Put a piece of wire through the center and twist it tightly at the back of the bow to hold all the loops together. The wire should be tight enough so that the loops move

independently and can be adjusted to create a full, fluffy bow.

6 Spread out the bow loops by pulling the second loop on one side away from you and the third loop on that side toward you. The fourth loop remains in the center. Repeat on the other side of the bow. Trim the ends of the tails even.

LAYERED BOW
Bottom Bow

1 Measure the length of ribbon for the first tail. Hold the ribbon with your thumb and forefinger.

2 Make a loop with the right side of the ribbon facing out.

3 Make a full twist of the ribbon so the right side of the ribbon is still facing out, and make a loop toward the other side.

4 Continue making loops right and left, fully twisting the ribbon before making each loop, until you have made six loops. Wrap a piece of florist wire around the center and twist it tightly at the back of the bow. The wire should be loose enough so the loops move independently and can be adjusted to make a full, fluffy bow yet tight enough to hold the bow together. Pull the loops apart to make a round bow.

Top Bow

5 Repeat steps 1-3, only make the second bow slightly smaller than the first one, make eight loops instead of six, and don't add the wire.

6 To make a center loop, twist the remaining ribbon around your thumb. Place a piece of florist wire through the loop and twist it in back of the bow. Pull the loops apart.

7 Wire the bows together.

Note: Use a curling iron on a low setting to revive a tired bow.

HORIZONTAL

Materials

- *11"x5"x4" (White) ceramic vase*
- *1 Floral foam (green)*
- *8 Stems (yellow) sunflowers*
- *5 Sprays (orange) black-eyed Susans (3 flowers each)*
- *5 Sprays (yellow) mini daisies*
- *3 Sprays (beige) baby's breath*

Tools

- *Wire cutters*
- *Tape measure*
- *Hot glue gun/glue sticks*

Note: Insert all the stems 1-2" into the foam. Completed project is 25"x13"x10" tall

Instructions

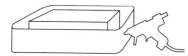

1 Floral foam. Hot glue the foam to the bottom of the vase.

2 Sunflowers. Cut all the stems to 9" tall. (Measure from the top of the flower head.)

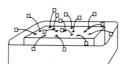

3 Black-eyed Susans. Cut the sprays into three 9" tall flowers.

4 Mini daisies. Cut each spray into two stems. Cut two stems to 12" tall and the remaining stems to 8" tall.

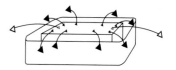

5 Baby's breath. Cut each spray into three 9" stems.

VERTICAL

Materials

- 11"x 6"x 4" Tall (white) basket
- 2 Floral foams (green)
- Sphagnum moss
- Floral pins

Silk flowers

- 1 Bush rex begonia leaves (12 stems)
- 1 Bush silver queen leaves (16 stems)
- 1 Spray Virginia creeper
- 1 Spray grape leaves
- 1 Spray mini ivy
- 6 Stems (purple) bells of Ireland
- 1 Stem (pink) scabiosa (3 flowers each)
- 3 Stems (purple) scabiosa (3 flowers each)

Tools

- Wire cutters
- Tape measure

Note: Insert all stems 3-4" into the foam. Completed project is 22"x26"x27" tall.

Instructions

1 Floral foam. Place foam on end, side by side in the basket. Secure the foam together with floral pins.

2 Rex begonia bush and Silver queen bush. Rex is 18" tall and queen is 16" tall.

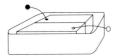

3 Virginia creeper, Grape leaf and Mini ivy. All are 12" tall

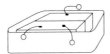

4 Bells of Ireland. Cut three stems to 22" tall, and three stems to 17" tall.

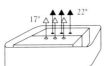

5 Pink scabiosa. Cut the flowers into single 14", 14", and 12" stems.

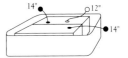

6 Purple scabiosa. Cut the stems to 18", 16" and 12"; 9", 9" and 9"; 11", 10" and 10" tall.

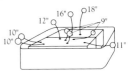

7 Moss. Cover foam with moss. Secure with floral pins.

TRIANGULAR

Materials

- *12" Tall 6" diameter round vase*
- *1 Floral foam (green)*

Silk flowers

- *3 Stems (peach) bells of Ireland*
- *2 Stems (pink) liatris*
- *3 Stems (pink) lilac*
- *6 Stems (white) dogwood*
- *1 Stem (pink) mini delphinium*
- *2 Stems open (peach) roses*
- *1 Stem weeping willow*
- *1 Spray trailing ivy*
- *1 Spray Virginia creeper*

Tools

- *Wire cutters*
- *Serrated knife*

Note: Insert the bells of Ireland, roses and weeping willow 5-6" into the foam. Insert the rest of the flowers and leaves 2-3". Completed project is 31" high 22" wide

Instructions

1 Foam. Insert full foam block into container and trim excess top 2" above the rim of the vase.

2 Bells of Ireland. All are 22" tall. Bend into curves and insert 5" into foam.

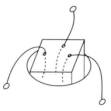

3 Roses. Cut stems to 12" and 10" tall. Bend flowers forward, insert 5" into foam.

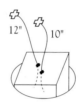

4 Liatris. Cut stems to 23 and 22" tall. Insert 3" into foam.

5 Lilac. All are 12" tall. Insert 2" into foam.

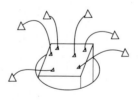

6 Dogwood. All are 12" tall. Insert 3" into foam.

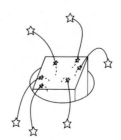

7 Delphinium. Cut to 17" tall. Insert 5" into foam.

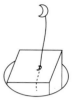

8 Ivy. Cut off two 19" long stems, and save the remaining spray for other arrangements. Insert 2" into foam.

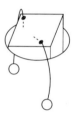

9 Virginia creeper. Cut off two 17" long stems (save the remaining spray for other arrangements). Insert 2" into foam.

10 Weeping willow. Leave stem the full length (36" long). Insert 5" into foam.

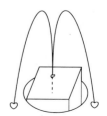

OVAL

Materials

- 13" Wide 9" tall (white) round ceramic urn
- 2 Floral foam (green)
- Floral pins

Silk flowers

- 9 Stems (golden) sunflowers
- 6 Stems (yellow) zinnias
- 12 Stems (blue) sweet peas
- 7 Stems (yellow) statice
- 8 Stems (yellow) mini daisies
- 6 Stems (off-white) baby's breath

Tools

- Wire cutters
- Tape measure

Note: Insert stems 2-3" into foam. Completed project is 27"x23" tall.

Instructions

1 Floral foam. Place side by side and secure with floral pins. Wedge into container.

2 Sunflowers. Cut one stem to 18" and the rest to 12" tall.

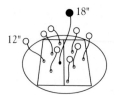

3 Zinnias. Cut stems to 14" tall.

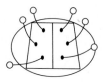

4 Sweet peas. Cut stems to 17" tall.

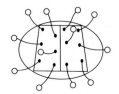

5 Statice. Cut all statice into two stems; 10" and 8" tall.

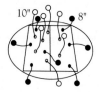

6 Mini daisies. Cut all mini daisies into two stems; 13" and 7" tall.

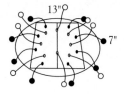

7 Baby's breath. Cut all baby's breath into two stems; 20" and 8" tall.

MINIMAL

Materials

- 7" Square, 6" tall (deep pink) vase
- 1 Floral foam (green)
- 1 Oz. sphagnum moss
- Floral pins

Silk flowers

- 6 Stems (red) roses
- 4 Stems (purple) statice
- 4 Stems (pink and blue) mini daisies

Tools

- Wire cutters
- Serrated knife
- Hot glue gun/glue sticks

Note: Insert roses and statice 3" into foam and the mini daisies 2". Completed project is 26" tall 9" wide

Instructions

1 Foam. Cut a 5" X 4" X 3" piece of foam. Glue the foam to the bottom of the vase.

2 Roses. Cut the flowers to 14", 16", 16", 16", 20" and 22" tall.

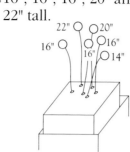

3 Statice. Spread the flowers and cut the statice to 9", 11", 18" and 18" tall.

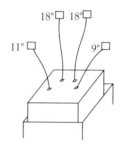

4 Mini daisies. All are 9" tall. Bend into graceful curves.

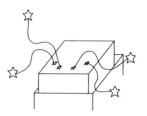

5 Sphagnum moss. Cover the foam with pieces of moss. Secure moss with floral pins.

45

"S" CURVE

Materials

- 4" Tall 5" wide, round (blue) vase
- 1 Floral foam (green)
- Floral pins

Silk Flowers

- 3 Stems (mauve) delphiniums
- 2 Stems (lavender) hydrangeas
- 3 Stems (blue) lilac
- 1 Stem (pink) lilac
- 5 Stems (mauve) mini lilies

Tools

- Wire cutters
- Serrated knife

Note: Insert all the flowers 3" into the foam. Completed arrangement is 9" Tall 15" wide

Instructions

1 Foam. Cut the foam to extend an inch above the rim and fit snugly in the vase.

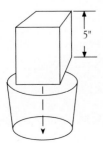

2 Delphiniums. Two are 16" tall; one is 15". Bend the stems before placing.

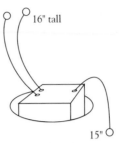

3 Hydrangeas. Both are 6" tall.

4 Pink and blue lilacs. Pink is 5" tall; blue are 9", 6" and 6" tall.

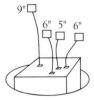

5 Mini lilies. All are 9" tall.

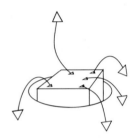

FREE FORM

Materials

- *10"x4" Tall round (red vase)*
- *1 Floral foam*
- *Floral pins*

Silk flowers

- *12 Stems (blue) hydrangeas*
- *5 Stems (peach) mini delphiniums*
- *3 Stems (pink) mini delphiniums*
- *6 Stems (blue) baby's breath*

Tools

- *Wire cutters*
- *Measuring tape*

Note: Insert all flowers stems 2-3" into foam. Completed project is 29"x18" tall

Instructions

1. Floral foam. Wedge the full block of foam (wide side down) into the container.

2. Hydrangeas. All are 13" tall.

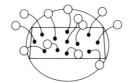

3. Peach and pink mini delphiniums. All are 16" tall.

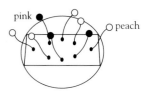

4. Baby's breath. Cut into three stems each; 11", 8", and 8" tall.

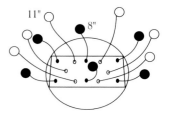

CRESCENT SHAPED

Materials

- 9" X 6" X 1½" tall (pink) vase
- 1 Floral foam (green)
- 1 Oz. sphagnum moss
- Floral pins

Silk flowers

- 2 Stems (white) bells of Ireland
- 1 Spray mini ivy
- 2 Stems hydrangeas
- 2 Stems (peach) open roses
- 2 Stems (peach) rose buds

Tools

- Serrated knife to cut foam
- Wire cutters
- Hot glue gun/glue sticks

Note: Insert all stems the full depth of the foam. Completed project is 14" high 16" wide.

Instructions

1 Foam. Cut foam to 6 ½" X 3 ½" X 3". Glue foam to bottom of vase.

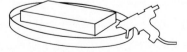

2 Bells of Ireland. Both are 16" tall. Cut one flower into thirds (5", 5", and 6" tall). Leave remaining flower whole, bend into curve, and place in foam.

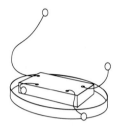

3 Hydrangeas. Cut flowers to 9" and 6" tall.

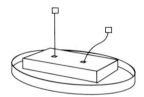

4 Open roses. Both are 7" tall. Bend flowers forward.

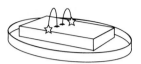

5 Rose buds. Both are 7" tall. Insert at angles.

6 Mini ivy. Cut two 9" stems. (Save remainder of spray for other arrangements.)

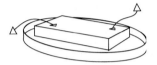

7 Moss. Cover foam with bits of moss at the base of the stems.

48

DRIED CENTERPIECE

Materials

- 6" (Brown) fireside basket
- Floral foam

Dried Flowers

- 3 Stems (white) peonies
- 12 Stems (white and pink) roses
- 10 Stems (lavender) phlox
- 8 Stems (blue) delphiniums
- 10 Stems (yellow) narcissus
- 12 (Green) salal leaves
- 5 Stems (mauve) baby's breath
- 5 Stems (blue-grey) latifolia

Tools

- Scissors
- Tape measure
- Hot glue gun/glue sticks

Note: Insert stems 1-2" into foam. Completed project is 17"x12"x8" tall

Instructions

1. Floral foam. Cut 2" piece from end of foam, and hot glue to bottom of basket.

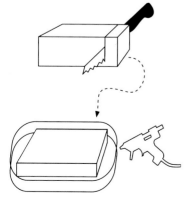

2. Peonies, Roses, Phlox. Cut all to 5" tall.

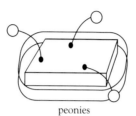

peonies

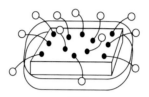

roses

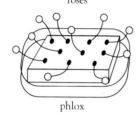

phlox

3. Delphiniums. Cut the delphinium stem (from under the bottom bloom) to 3" long.

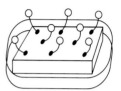

4. Narcissus and salal leaves. Cut the narcissus stems to 5". Hot glue flowers and leaves throughout the basket, in-between the other flowers.

5. Latifolia and baby's breath. Cut into 3" clusters, and hot glue throughout the flowers.

Dried Floral Arrangement

Materials

- 6" Round (natural) French basket with handle
- Floral foam

Dried flowers

- 2 Stems (Purple) liatris
- 5 Stems (blue) larkspur
- 10 Stems (red and burgundy) roses
- 15 Stems (pink) asters
- 3 Stems (pink) wheat celosia
- 6 Stems (blue) delphinium
- 10 Stems (yellow) solidaster
- 10 Stems (purple) statice
- 5 Stems (lavender) statice
- 6 Stems (blue-grey) latifolia
- 6 Stems (white) baby's breath

Tools

- Scissors
- Tape measure
- Hot glue gun/glue sticks

Note: Insert stems 1" into foam. Completed project is 23"x15" tall.

Instructions

1 Foam. Cut the foam in half. Glue ½ piece in bottom of basket.

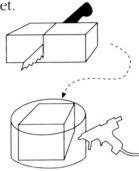

2 Liatris. Cut stems to 8" tall.

3 Larkspur. Cut the stems from beneath the bottom blooms to 4".

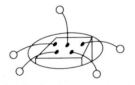

4 Roses, asters, wheat celosia. Cut to 8" tall.

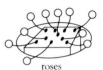
roses

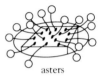
asters

wheat celosia

5 Delphiniums and solidaster. Break them into 12" pieces, and hot glue throughout arrangement.

6 Latifolia, statice and baby's breath. Break into 3" sections, and hot glue throughout the arrangement.

DECORATOR BASKET

Materials

- 8"x15"x4" Tall (white) basket with handle

- 1 Floral foam (green)

Silk flowers

- 7 Stems (fuchsia) dahlias

- 6 Stems (indigo) ranunculas

- 10 Stems (white) dogwood

- 6 Stems (pink) field flowers

Tools

- Wire cutters

- Serrated knife

- Hot glue gun/glue

Note: Insert all flowers 2-3" into foam. Completed project is 16" tall 20" wide

Instructions

1 Foam. Glue the bottom of the foam to the bottom of the basket

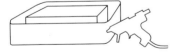

2 Dahlias. All are 8" tall.

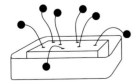

3 Ranunculas Cut all the ranunculas into two single stems each: one 10" tall bloom and bud and one single 8" tall stem.

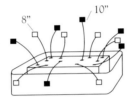

4 Dogwood. Cut the flowers into two sprays each: 11" tall and 10" tall.

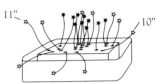

5 Field flowers. All are 12" tall.

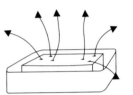

Magnolia Arrangement

Materials

- *10"x3" Round (blue) ceramic vase*
- *Floral foam*
- *Spanish moss*
- *Floral pins*

Silk flowers

- *2 Stems (white) magnolias*
- *3 Stems (blue) lilac (2 flowers each)*
- *6 Pieces floral stem wire*

Tools

- *Wire cutters*
- *Tape measure*
- *Hot glue gun/glue sticks*

Note: Insert flowers the full depth of foam. Insert leaves 1-2". Completed project is 13"x15" tall.

Instructions:

1 Foam. Insert end of foam inside vase, and cut off top leaving 1-2" above the rim of the vase. Hot glue foam to bottom of vase.

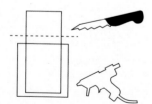

2 Magnolias. Cut to 14" and 12" tall.

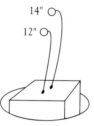

3 Magnolia leaves. Cut eight leaves from cut stems. Wrap floral stem wire around ends of leaves to lengthen stems.

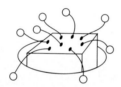

4 Lilacs. Cut into separate 10" and 8" flowers.

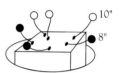

5 Moss. Cover foam with pieces of moss. Secure with floral pins.

Red Lily Arrangement

Materials

- *11" X 2" Tall (bronze) round vase (diameter of opening is 3")*
- *Floral foam*
- *1 Oz. sphagnum moss*
- *Floral pins*

Silk flowers

- *4 Stems (ruby red) lilies*
- *4 Stems (yellow) mini orchids*

Tools

- *Wire cutters*
- *Serrated knife*
- *Hot glue gun/glue sticks*

Note: All flowers are inserted 2" into foam. Completed project is 23" high 22" wide

Instructions

1 Foam. Cut a 3" X 3" X 4" piece of foam (or one to fit the opening of your vase and extend 1-2" above the rim. Glue the the foam to the bottom of the vase.

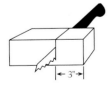

2 Lilies. Cut three lilies to 16",18" and 21" tall. Cut the fourth lily into two 7" flowers and one 11" tall bud.

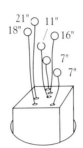

3 Mini Orchids. All are 18" tall. Bend into graceful curves.

4 Moss. Cover the foam with moss, and secure with floral pins.

WILD POPPIES

Materials

- 12" (Dark green) oval basket
- Floral foam

Silk flowers

- 18 Picks (variegated) mini oak ivy foliage
- 6 Sprays (white) mini daisies
- 14 Stems (red) poppies

Tools

- Wire cutters
- Hot glue gun/glue sticks
- Tape measure

Note: Insert stems 2" into foam. Completed project is 24"x18"x14" tall.

Instructions

1 Foam. Hot glue one full block of foam to the bottom of the basket.

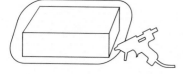

2 Oak ivy. Insert full picks.

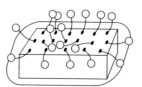

3 Mini daisies. Cut all stems into three 10" sprays.

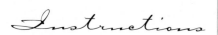

4 Poppies. Cut all stems to 12" tall.

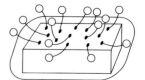

Dazzling Floral Arrangement

Materials

- 6" High 10" wide, (white) round basket with handle
- 2 Floral foam (green)
- Floral wire (light weight)

Silk flowers

- 1 Bush begonia leaves
- 8 Stems (pink) sweet Williams
- 14 Stems (yellow) mini lilies
- 8 Stems (pink) field flowers
- 4 Stems (yellow) statice

Tools

- Wire cutters
- Hot glue gun/glue sticks
- Tape measure

Note: Insert all flowers 2-3" into foam. Completed project is 21" tall 20" wide

Instructions

1 Foam. Hot glue one foam to the bottom of the basket. Hot glue second foam on top of first foam.

2 Begonia bush. Cut two 22" long stems from the bush (save the rest for other arrangements). Insert in foam, and wind around handle as shown. Secure with 6" pieces of floral wire every four inches or so.

3 Sweet Williams. All are 14" tall.

4 Field flowers. Cut each spray into two 14" tall stems.

5 Mini lilies. All are 15" tall.

6 Statice. All are 14" tall.

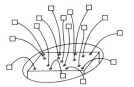

Materials

- 4 1/2" X 11" X 7" Tall (white) basket with handle
- 1 Floral foam (green)

Silk Flowers

- 7 Stems (white) open roses
- 12 Stems (pink) Peruvian lilies
- 6 Stems (purple) statice

Tools

- Wire cutters
- Hot glue gun/glue sticks
- Tape measure

Insert all flowers 3" into foam. Completed project is 15" tall 23" wide

Instructions

1 Foam. Glue foam to bottom of basket.

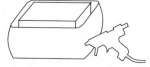

2 Roses. All are 13" tall. Bend stems into curves.

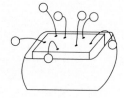

3 Peruvian lilies. Cut the flowers into two sprays each: 13" and 7" tall.

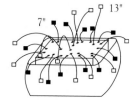

4 Statice. All flowers are 11" tall. Spread the blossoms before inserting them in foam.

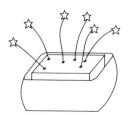

BASKET OF VIOLETS

Materials

- *10"x6"x5" Tall (brown) basket*
- *Floral foam*

Silk flowers

- *5 Bushes (lavender) violets (10 stems each)*

Tools

- *Wire cutters*
- *Hot glue gun/glue sticks*

Note: Insert the stems 1-2" into foam. Completed project is 14"x10"x13" tall.

Instructions

1. Foam. Hot glue the foam to the bottom of the basket.

2. Violets. All are 9" tall.

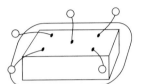

Materials

- 9" Tall 5" wide (green) round vase
- 1 Floral foam (green)

Silk Flowers

- 5 Stems (pink) snapdragons
- 3 Stems (pink) open roses
- 4 Stems (white) mini daisies
- 2 Stems (lavender) scabiosa
- 1 Spray mini ivy
- 1 Stem weeping willow

Tools

- Wire cutters
- Serrated knife

Completed project is 27" high 26" wide

Instructions

1 Foam. Insert the end of the foam block into the vase, and push it to fit snuggly in side the container. Cut the top off evenly, leaving an inch or so above the rim.

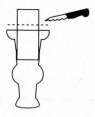

2 Snapdragons. All are 21" tall. Bend four into graceful curves before inserting them 4" into the foam.

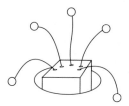

3 Roses. Cut flowers to 14", 15" and 17" tall. Bend the heads forward and insert 4" into foam.

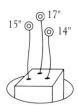

4 Mini daisies. Cut the flowers into two sprays each: 7" and 18" tall. Curve the stems that droop and insert the flowers 2-3" into the foam.

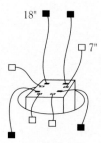

5 Scabiosa. Cut the flowers into two single stems each: 15" and two 8" tall stems. Insert 2-3" into foam.

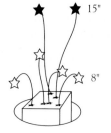

6 Mini ivy. Cut two 12" stems and two 8" stems from the spray and insert 2" into foam.

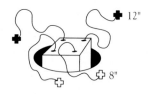

7 Weeping willow. Leave stem full length, and insert 4" into foam. Arrange branches as per photo.

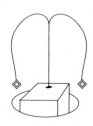